Astral Projection

A Complete Guide to Astral Travel and Out of Body Experiences

Jamie Parr

Table of Contents

Introduction

Astral projection, sometimes called astral travel, is an intentional out of body experience (OBE.) Those who engage in astral projection believe in the existence of a soul or a sense of consciousness that is separate from the physical body, which is referred to as the astral body. This astral body is capable of traveling outside of, or away from, the physical body, which is how astral projection or astral travel is achieved.

In this book, we are going to discuss this phenomenon, including how you can begin to astral project and astral travel yourself! It is important to understand that astral projection is something that should not be completed until you know what you are doing. While many will have an unintentional OBE, if you do intend to have an OBE and plan on using it for any specific purpose, you need to know how to do so safely. As with all things spiritual, knowing how to start and stop an experience is important as it creates the opportunity for you to engage in that experience in a protected manner.

I encourage you to first read through this entire book before engaging in any sort of astral projection or traveling experience. That way, you will be fully aware of what it takes, and will be able to set yourself up for a positive experience. Once you know how to safely astral project, the experiences you are capable of having are phenomenal. Astral projection and travel can be used for everything from visiting other realms or visiting different areas of earth without physically going there, to performing energy work on yourself in a deeply spiritual way. There are many ways that you can use astral projection and travel to your advantage, especially once you are fully aware of what you are doing and how to do it safely.

Thank you for taking the time to read this book, I hope you thoroughly enjoy learning about astral projection!

Chapter 1: What Is Astral Projection?

Astral projection is, as you likely know, a form of OBE where the astral body is projected away from the physical body. Although the term was only coined in the 19th century, it has been happening for many centuries within cultures from all around the world. In different cultures throughout history, astral projection was seen as being an opportunity to connect with God-like beings, to connect with people in another realm, to perform tasks that were impossible for the human body, to collect information, and much more. Many believed that once someone passed into the afterlife, they could use astral projection as a way to present themselves to people on earth, using this as a way to visit and send messages from the other side. Others believed that you could only use your astral body on earth if you were physically present on earth and routinely used it as a way to perform tasks on earth, such as to communicate with people far away or find information that was otherwise hidden. Now that the world is much more interconnected and information is widely shared, we have a much clearer understanding of what is truly possible through astral projection.

The Science of Astral Projection

To date, there is no scientific evidence that there is a soul separate of the body or that the soul can separate from the body to perform astral projection or astral travel. This science has been performed by monitoring neural activity within the brain and has discovered that neural activity remains the same during an astral projection as it does at any other time.

Despite the fact that science has not confirmed the ability for astral projection to take place, many are confident that this is precisely what is happening. Based on mutual experiences that many have had, they are confident that astral projection is real, and science has simply not found a way to properly measure the experience, yet. Those who firmly believe in science yet have no way of confirming or proving the existence of astral projection, will often use hallucinations as a way to describe what is happening.

Astral Projection in Different Cultures

Astral projection, or some form of it, has been identified in historical reports related to the Western world, Biblical times, ancient Egypt, China, Hinduism in India, Japan, Inuit Nunangat, and the Amazon. Each of these historical reports has its own unique take on what astral projection is, why it was used, and what the encounters meant.

In the Western world, during the medieval and renaissance times, it was believed that the astral body was an intermediate body of light that linked a rational soul to the physical body. In other words, the astral body does not represent the soul itself, but the link between the two. It was believed that this created the link between Heaven and Earth, and that the astral body and astral planes are composed of the spheres of the planets and stars. It was said that these areas of the astral world are populated by demons, angels, and a variety of different spirits.

In Biblical accounts, it was believed that the astral body was a subtle body attached to the physical body using a silver cord. The belief is that, when you go to Heaven, the cord breaks, permanently detaching your astral body from the physical body and granting you the freedom to go to Heaven or Hell. They claimed this cord was connected to the spine, while many claimed the spine itself is the silver cord.

In ancient Egypt, soul travel was depicted as a way for the spiritual body to disconnect from the physical body. While we do not entirely understand why this happened or what it represents, we do know that many visual accounts or pictures from that time show Gods hovering over the bodies of the dead, using their astral body to exist in that space.

In China, Taoist alchemical practice involves people creating an energy body using specific breathing meditations. These breathing meditations are said to draw energy into the body, where the Taoist then draws it into a pearl, that is then circulated throughout the body. As the pearl reaches maturity, the individual is able to subtly release themselves from their body to exist in a purely energetic state. Some would use this energy body as a way to appear in many places at once, providing them with the opportunity to talk to many people, spread a single message quickly, or call people to travel to them.

In Hinduism, the astral body was seen as being a way for individuals to connect with God-like energies, as well as the energies of their gurus. Individuals who were meditating or practicing yoga, or occasionally those who were going about their day to day life, would receive astral projections of a specific god or their guru when something important was going on. For example, a god may appear when they are in need of specific protection, or their guru may appear when they are ready to learn the next stage of their spiritual journey, or when trouble appeared. In Hinduism, it is believed that only those who are master yoga practitioners can experience astral projection, so it is commonly accepted that the average person cannot achieve this.

In Japan, astral projection was often used as a force of evil, where people would target or direct hate or harm toward anyone that they were holding a grudge against. They also believed that souls would leave a living body if the body were extremely sick or comatose because the body was no longer safe or inhabitable for that soul. By leaving the body, the soul was able to protect itself, but it was also believed that the body was left open to harm from other entities.

Inuit First Nations were said to be able to travel to remote locations using astral projection, and they could report their experiences to fellow members of the community. For example, they would be able to bring back information about how abundant a hunt would be, how to stop bad luck during a hunt, how to cure a sick person, among other pieces of information that were unavailable to "normal" people. These individuals were often highly respected and valued members of the community. Often, these abilities were said to be passed down through lineage.

In the Amazon, astral projection was used as a way to heal, consult cosmological beings, name newborn babies, pray for an abundant harvest, or to get the help of other beings. There, it was called "soul flight," as they believed the soul would fly away from the body to retrieve this information from the cosmos.

Chapter 2: Astral Projection Vs. Astral Traveling

Astral projection and astral travel are two entirely different terms, though the terms are often used interchangeably. While the experience of projecting out of the body and existing in the physical realm remains the same, the energy it takes and the level of protection that is required varies depending on what type of astral experience you intend on having.

Knowing what you intend to do with your astral experience determines whether you need to prepare for astral projection, or for astral travel. This way, you can take the necessary measures of protection to keep your mind, body, emotions, and spirit safe from anything that may be lurking in the astral realms.

The Experience of Astral Projection

Astral projection is an experience where you project your astral body out of your physical body. This is often used as a way to manifest in one place, or many places, in the same space time continuum that your physical body exists in. Your goal is not to move around or venture anywhere; instead, your goal is to appear in a single space. For example, you might astral project into the room you are presently in, or you might astral project into someone else's room or house if you want to talk to or connect with someone.

This is generally where people will begin their astral journey, as astral projection is far easier and safer than astral travel. Since you are only going to one location, or perhaps several locations but without the intention of moving far, and with one specific purpose, you can achieve this far more easily than astral travel.

The Experience of Astral Travel

Astral travel is similar to astral projection, except that there is a form of traveling involved. Unlike projection, which is more static, astral travel includes moving through time and space, in a way that is detached from your physical body. For example, you might astral travel back through time, into the future, or to a different planet or realm as an opportunity to experience a different space or gain information from a different time and space location.

Astral travel takes far more effort because you need to be able to maintain your astral projection long enough to physically move around. You also need to be able to protect yourself, as you become more susceptible to dangers and psychic attack when you are moving through the space time continuum or venturing into other realms.

How Each State Is Achieved

Both astral projection and astral travel are achieved by first reaching a deep state of meditation. You may like to use yoga, first, as a way to increase your relaxation and prime yourself for the experience. Other's will use energy healing or energy work as a way to prepare their energy body for the experience. It is important that you also mentally, emotionally, and physically prepare yourself for the spiritual journey by anchoring yourself into the present space.

Before you can astral project or astral travel, you must be relaxed and detached enough to release your astral body from your physical body. Any level of force, pressure, or effort to control the situation excessively will prevent your astral body from leaving your physical body. You need to be able to create a sense of detachment so the astral body can safely and effectively remove itself from the physical body and have an astral experience. Excessive control, force, or pressure from you on a mental or emotional level will actually cause you to cling to your physical body, as these conditions make it unsafe for your astral body to be separated from it. Your astral body will not leave your physical body if it knows that your physical body is not ready for the possibility of your astral body not returning.

Chapter 3: Astral Projection and Your Third Eye

Your third eye is largely responsible for your ability to astral project as it provides you with the opportunity to experience the unseen. Attempting to astral project or travel before you have awakened your third eye is not ideal, as you will not able to freely interact with the realms you will project into and travel through otherwise. There are many ways you can safely, comfortably awaken your third eye. In fact, I have an entire book titled *Third Eye Awakening* that can help you with this very task.

Anytime you work with astral projection or travel, you should be ready to work with your third eye, too. The energy you perceive, experience, and possibly bring back with you will be recognized and experienced through your third eye first. For example, if an entity attaches to you when you are astral traveling, you will perceive that with your third eye immediately upon returning, assuming your third eye is awakened and properly scanning your energy. If your third eye is not awake or is awake but not balanced, you might miss the signs that you have brought an energy or entity back with you and find yourself having physical, mental, or emotional manifestations of that energy or entity. We will discuss more about how you can recognize this and protect yourself against it in Chapter 5.

Preparing Your Third Eye for OBE

Just as you need to prepare your mind, emotions, and physical body for astral projection, you also need to prepare your third eye. Unlike your mind, emotions, and body, which can be prepared on the same day as your astral experience, your third eye needs to be prepared well in advance, leading up to your experience. You can prepare your third eye through meditation, balancing it, and priming it through nourishing foods. Rituals involving essential oils and yoga can also be used to help balance your third eye, as well as a reiki or energy healing session if need be. You should also feel comfortable using your clair senses before you astral project, as your clair senses will be helpful in navigating the astral realm safely.

You will know you are ready for astral travel when you feel comfortable working with your third eye and your clair senses. You should also feel comfortable completely cleansing your third eye and grounding yourself from unwanted energetic experiences, as these will be made far more intense by astral travel. While you are not guaranteed to pick up unwanted energies or entities, it is possible. Knowing how to remove these energies or, balance yourself until someone else can remove these energies, is important. Not knowing how to do this can lead to overwhelming or unwanted experiences, which may make it more complicated for you to travel in the future or, may create discomfort during other energetic and spiritual experiences.

It is important that you do not rush your OBE or your astral experiences, as the slower and steadier you go, the stronger your ability to protect yourself will be. This way, you are far more likely to have a positive and enjoyable experience, rather than a traumatic or negative one.

Creating Your Astral Portal

One excellent part of working with your third eye is that, before you work with your astral body, you can work with astral energy by creating your own personal portal. Your portal is essentially the energetic "space" you will use to move into your astral body and detach your astral body from your physical body. Many people who regularly engage in astral projection or travel will create their own energy portal, which is specifically designed to help protect and cleanse their energies as they leave and return to their physical bodies. This is done by using personal intentions, specific energy codes, and other energetic manipulations to create a space that nurtures your spiritual self.

If you wish to create your own astral portal, you can do so by meditating and using your third eye to design the portal. The easiest way is to visualize an energy space in front of you and to set the intention for this energy space to lead you to the astral realm. You can then design the space as you wish, using colors intended to cleanse and protect, and by adding symbols and designs that create a cleansing and protecting energy.

It is helpful to come back to your astral portal regularly to replenish the energy, reinforce the symbolism and energy field, and to become used to this particular energy space. The more comfortable you become with visiting this portal and working with the energy, the easier it will be for you to rely on it. Further, this helps you grow acquainted with the energy that is associated with the astral realm and makes it easier for you to feel comfortable working within the astral space.

Perceiving the Energy Around You

Your third eye is responsible for your clair senses, and your clair senses are responsible for helping you navigate the unseen world. When you astral project, things feel different from moving through the physical world because you are using a different body to do it. Having your clair senses activated and being particularly skilled with and comfortable using at least one or two of your clair senses ensures that you are able to perceive the energy around you during astral projection or astral travel.

As you embark on your astral projection experiences, you will have the opportunity to work with energy in a unique way. If you are comfortable using your clair senses, then you will have an easier time working with this energy and recognizing where it comes from, how it is unique from energy in the physical plane, and how this energy can be used.

Chapter 4: Benefits and Uses for Astral Projection

Aside from being enjoyable or offering you a unique skillset, astral projection actually brings many wonderful benefits with it. Once you have learned how to properly engage in astral projection, there are many things to be gained from this unique ability. You can use these benefits independently, or together with each other, as an opportunity to make astral projection even more useful.

Improves Your Focus

An excellent benefit that exists both during astral projection and during your waking life is improved focus. In order to astral project, and especially to astral travel, you require a great deal of focus to help you maintain your astral experience. You need to be focused enough to meditate, remove your astral self from your physical body, and project it into astral space. You will also need a great deal of focus to travel through astral space and time.

As you continue to improve your focus on astral projection or travel, you will find that this focus benefits you in many other ways, too. The ability to focus is a skill, and it can be used in any area of your life. With an enhanced ability to focus, you can work on tasks or projects more efficiently, meditate for longer periods of time, and focus intently on caring for yourself and your energy. The more focused you can be, the better you can cleanse and protect yourself, and the better your energetic experiences will be, whether it is using your clair senses or astral projecting or traveling.

Improved focus works both ways, too. In addition to astral projection improving your focus, you can also use other focus building practices to help you improbe your ability to astral project.

Improves Your Ability to Enjoy Life

There is more to life than what we see with our physical eyes or feel with our physical senses. When you limit your life to purely what exists in the physical, you cut yourself off from many things that exist for your pleasure. Those who play in the astral realm using astral projection or travel realize that there is far more to life. They enjoy a whole range of phenomenal experiences beyond the physical body.

As you engage in astral projection, you will find yourself eliminating unnecessary distractions so you can instead focus on the goal of your astral journey, which allows for more pure and intense experiences.

Many people report that after learning how to astral travel, their physical experiences are enhanced as well because they find themselves experiencing far more than just what they see in the physical at any given moment. For example, the simple experience of drinking your favorite drink can bring with it far more enjoyment because you are experiencing the energy on top of the physical experience itself, too. This often never goes away, meaning all of your experiences, Earthly and otherwise, will be intensified.

Increases the Quality of Your Relationships

Relationships in your life are experienced through physical senses and connections, as well as through spiritual senses and connections. Learning how to work with your astral body means you discover new ways to connect with other people in your life because you become aware of their astral body, too. You begin to recognize that there are many ways that you connect with and relate to others, and those multiple layers of connection can deepen the quality of relationships you share with others.

The ability to create a spiritual connection with people through your astral bodies means you can deepen the level of intimacy between yourself and others. Reading that person's energy and associating with them in any way, whether it be physical or beyond, becomes far more powerful because you find yourself understanding that individual on a deeper level. Through this, you feel an increased sense of compassion, empathy, and closeness toward the other individual. You also find yourself appreciating them and their presence more, allowing you to stop taking others for granted as you gain more out of your relationships.

Empowers You in a Unique Way

Being able to astral project or travel actually creates a deep level of empowerment in anyone who engages in these particular skills. Realizing that you have the power to exist beyond your body and interact with things beyond your physical self creates a sense that you can handle anything. You experience increased confidence and self-esteem as you realize that your abilities are far greater than you ever imagined, and you are more powerful than you previously thought.

For people who tend to find themselves feeling a lack of self-confidence or self-esteem, or who generally find themselves feeling incapable of handling new challenges, astral projection can help. Through your deepened abilities and increased trust in yourself, you begin to believe that you can handle anything that comes your way. Further, your increased ability to sense and navigate Earthly experiences also improves your sense of self-confidence and self-esteem as you will find that fewer things seem uncertain. For example, you no longer have to worry about what other people are feeling because your ability to read energy means you can detect anytime the energy becomes unfavorable for you or your safety. Thus, you do not need to worry because your intuition is stronger, and your ability to protect yourself is increased.

Helps you Tap into Specific Knowledge

Astral projection has often been used as a way to tap into specific knowledge from the cosmos, gods, ethereal energies or entities, or even people that are physically far away but capable of providing the help you need. In various cultures, astral projection was used to present oneself to an individual who would be capable of helping so that the individual could be "called" to the physical location of the person seeking help. It was also used to consult with cosmic energies as a way to find out information about anything they may have been wondering about. Missing persons were located, necessary healing guidance was received, and even simple questions were answered through the cosmos. For many cultures, astral projecting oneself to the cosmos to ask the cosmic energies for guidance was the standard way for receiving your name or meeting your spirit guides that would support you as you venture through Earth. If you have specific knowledge you want to tap into, whether it be the truth about the universe or the realms you exist in, or about what to name someone or what a certain piece of energy may be, you can use astral projection to help you.

Chapter 5: Protection Methods

Before you ever consider leaving your physical body, it is imperative that you learn about important protection methods for both your physical and astral bodies. Protection methods are less about knowing how to stop an unwanted experience from happening, and more about knowing how to protect yourself against unwanted experiences. These experiences can be completely out of your control, so trying to avoid them altogether can be futile. While protection measures will not help you come back to your body if need be, they can be used to prevent you from becoming trapped outside of your body. They can also protect you from unwanted energies or entities attaching themselves to you.

Protecting yourself during astral projection or travel needs to occur on a physical, mental, emotional, and spiritual level. The experiences you have during astral journeys are beyond the body, which means some of your senses will be invoked in unique ways. If you do not adequately prepare yourself, you might find yourself having nightmares, traumatic flashbacks, physical pains, or other strange manifestations of your experience. Adequately preparing yourself ensures you return from your journey as positively and peacefully as you left, which keeps each of your experiences safe and enjoyable.

What you are Protecting Yourself Against

When you astral project, there are many different known and unknown energy sources and entities that you are protecting yourself against. Some of these you will be aware of when you prepare to embark on your astral journey, while others you will be unaware of. This is because the universe is so vast that, despite the number of people who have astral projected or traveled before you, not every possible threat has been identified and exposed. Generally, protecting yourself against *all* energies and entities ensures that absolutely nothing can attach itself to you and harm you.

Unwanted energies that might attach to you are different from entities as they do not take on an individual sense of identity or form. Instead, they take on a specific energy type, which means they can attach to anything, whether it be you or something you keep close to yourself. The energies most people are attempting to protect themselves from include those that induce fear, anxiety, anger, aggression, depression, or other generally troubling emotional experiences. However, it is also important to avoid allowing energies that drive euphoria, bliss, and other uplifting or positive yet addicting energies, as this is not supportive of your wellbeing, either. In many cases, these especially uplifting energies can cause just as much damage by distorting your understanding of the world around you and encouraging you to make poor choices.

Entities that might attach themselves to you could be anything from ghosts or spirits to demons or bad entities that wish to cause you harm. These entities will often attach themselves to your soul and will follow you through your waking life, as well as your sleeping life, often causing nightmares where they present themselves and torment you.

Again, not all energies or entities will be identifiable. It will not always be someone or something that is easy to recognize, and it may be something that you cannot even specifically identify once it has attached itself to you. Knowing how to eliminate *all* unwanted energies and entities, identifiable or not, is important as it ensures that no one slips through the radar and remains attached to you in spite of your efforts to eliminate it.

It is important to understand that these energies and entities can easily attach themselves to an astral projector or traveler, however it is extremely challenging and unlikely for them to attach themselves if you have adequately protected yourself. Further, if you do find that you have been attacked by an unwanted energy or entity, you *must not let fear win*. Fear is an active energy that these energies and entities will feed off of, and it will ultimately entrap you and keep you stuck with these unwanted beings. Learning how to keep yourself confident as you eliminate these unwanted energies and entities is essential, as confidence is where your power lies. A lack of confidence is where *their* power lies.

Tools for Protection

You need to protect yourself and your space during astral projection or travel, as both can expose you to unwanted energy and entities. Your physical body is an obvious target, but the room surrounding you is a lesser known target that many new astral projectors will not think about. You can think about your room as being your physical portal to your astral experience, while your astral portal you created with your third eye is the one that represents the astral part of your portal.

The tools you use to protect yourself and your space include intention, crystals, essential oils or incense, and a talisman. Your intention is something you should create for yourself, as the more personal it is, the better. You want your intention to be clear and thorough, as this ensures you do not leave space for unwanted energy or entities to come through. A great example would be "I intend to experience the astral realm through my astral body, and I intend to remain entirely independent of every energy, entity, and being that I may come across whether it be from the astral realm or beyond."

Crystals you can use to protect yourself include ametrine, angelite, apophyllite, and sapphire. Amethyst, smoky quartz, and obsidian are also excellent as they can help remove harmful or unwanted energies from your space.

Essential oils, including sage, rosemary, and lavender, are excellent for use with astral projection or travel. You can also use herbs like Mugwort, kava kava, or blue lotus. All of these will assist you in having a smoother experiencing exiting and returning to your physical body, while also forming a protective shield around you, so you have a safer experience. If you wish to use incense, burning sage is excellent as it encourages astral energy to flow, while protecting and purifying your energy during your astral projection and after.

Talismans are a highly personal item that can be created and used for astral projection and astral travel. To create a talisman, you can use a crystal, piece of wood, or another item that can be inscribed with specific symbols, drenched in specific oils, or is otherwise designed to keep you safe. Once you have made your talisman, you will want to bless it under an entire moon cycle, from the start of a full moon to the end of a new moon, to properly prepare it for your astral journey.

Having all of your tools ready and situated before you leave your physical body is important, as they cannot protect you if they are not around you. Often, the process of placing your tools will be used as a part of a protection ritual that prepares your mind, body, emotions, and energy for the upcoming experience.

Creating a Protection Ritual

A protection ritual is a ritual that includes placing your tools, setting your intention, and ensuring that the energy in your space and in your body and astral body, are ready for astral projection or astral travel.

You can start your protection ritual by gathering all of the tools and supplies you will use for your astral journey. This includes crystals, essential oils, incense, talismans, candles, and anything else you may wish to lay around your space. You might also want to use a blanket and a pillow, so you are comfortable as you embark on your journey.

Once you have gathered everything, you will want to place it around your space, starting at the door and working clockwise around your room, as this sets the energy in a positive way. You can lay crystals in corners, on shelves, and anywhere else you desire. Candles, incense sticks, and dots of protection oils can also be placed. Always work around the perimeter of the room first. Then, when you are done, you can work around the space where you will be sitting or lying as you embark on your astral journey. When you're ready, you can sit or lie down and place any tools upon yourself, such as a crystal grid, anointment oil, or your talisman.

As you place your protective tools around, ensure that you are speaking your intention into the space. Repeat it over and over like a mantra, ensuring that you are breathing protective and cleansing energy into your space. This ensures that you are creating a space that will be safe for you to astral project or travel from and to return to.

Cleansing Yourself Upon Return

As soon as you return from your astral projection, a secondary ritual is needed. The cleansing ritual ensures that you remove any unwanted energies or entities from your physical space, so you are able to resume your normal life without any unwanted attachments. You should always cleanse yourself first, then your space and your tools.

The first part of cleansing yourself should be done in the astral realm. Upon returning to your astral portal, visualize your portal cleansing and protecting you from anything that may have attempted to attach itself to you. Give yourself a few moments to breathe and relax in this space so you can experience total cleansing. As you come back into your physical body, maintain the same cleansing breath, and use it as a way to remove unwanted energies and entities from yourself and your space. As you exhale, feel everything unwanted being blown out and away from your space, and as you inhale, feel peaceful, pure energies coming back into your space. Practice this breath several times over, feeling your energy cleanse deeply.

Next, you can use cleansing tools like black tourmaline, black obsidian, clear quartz, rose quartz, or selenite as a way to help you cleanse your personal energy. You can do this by either massaging your aura with this crystal or holding it in your hand, and visualizing it absorbing all unwanted energies while purifying and replenishing the energies in your astral body. You may also want to play binaural beats or solfeggio frequencies, which are attuned to a cleansing tone to help vibrationally detach any unwanted energies from your astral body, aura, physical body, and space.

Continue cleansing yourself until you feel deeply cleansed. Attempting to limit your cleansing to a finite amount of time can result in you ending your cleansing session before it is complete, which can allow unwanted energies to remain attached to you.

If you have embarked on a particularly large astral projection journey, or if you are new to astral projection, you may want to book a reiki healing or other energy healing session for after you have finished your journey. Having an official session booked can help ensure that you have no energy left attached to your energy field, as you have a professional energy cleanser helping you. Over time, you may not require this energy healing session any longer as you learn how to do it yourself and grow more confident in your abilities.

Cleansing Your Protection Tools

Cleansing your protection tools is an important part of your protection ritual, too. You need to cleanse your crystals and talismans in particular, as they are the ones most likely to hold energy on them. Other items in your physical vicinity can be cleansed using incense and sound healing frequencies, as both will help detach and eliminate unwanted energies from everything in your physical space using a purifying approach.

For your crystals and talisman, smoke from incenses like sage can be used to help cleanse them of unwanted energies. You can also lay used crystals against a clear quartz, run them through purified water so long as they are a true crystal and not a mineral, or leave them in the sunlight or moonlight. Full moons and new moons, in particular, are the best times for cleansing your crystals as this is when the energies of the moon are strongest, which helps your crystals return to their natural energy, too.

You should always cleanse your tools before and after you use them, as this ensures that they are always operating with the purest possible energy, which keeps them ready for use. It also prevents accidental energy absorption of energies you do not want to be working with, which helps keep you safe.

Chapter 6: How to Perform Astral Projection

Astral projection can be performed in two specific ways, both of which require your physical body to enter a sort of "slumber." In one method, you are truly asleep; in the other, you enter a deep state of meditation, which tricks your body into feeling like it is asleep. It is ideal that you use the meditation method before the sleep method if you are new to astral projection, as this ensures that you are able to awaken yourself and cleanse yourself in a specific period of time. Otherwise, you might find yourself in your astral body for too long, which can be an uncomfortable experience if you're not prepared for it.

Meditation to Astral Project

Meditation is the safest way to astral project because you keep a certain level of consciousness awake in your body, and it is easier to awaken from meditation than it is to awaken from a deep slumber. Even though your meditation will be fixed to end at a specific time, it can be helpful to set an alarm that will sound after a certain period of time to ensure that you come back to your body when you intend to. This way, you can limit your experience and exposure to a safe amount of time.

When you meditate to astral project, you will not start with astral projection. Instead, you will meditate to cleanse your energy body and your third eye; then, you will move into an astral meditation. This ensures that your energy is ready for the astral projection or traveling experience you are preparing for. Regardless of how frequently you astral project or travel, you will always want to follow this procedure to ensure that you are taking adequate care of your energy.

Meditation as a way to astral travel is a highly traditional method, seen in nearly every cultural practice that includes astral projection or soul travel. The purpose of meditation is to allow your physical body to reach a state of slumber so that it stops demanding your active consciousness, which means your active consciousness is free to leave your body for astral projection or travel. If you are not yet capable of meditating for extended periods of time, you must learn how to meditate first, as this ensures that you are able to remain in a state of meditation long enough for your astral experience. Awakening too soon can lead to you missing out on the full extent of your astral journey. This is not an ideal experience but can be avoided by developing a regular meditation practice and growing comfortable with meditation before using it to embark on astral projection or travel journeys.

Astral Projection and Sleep

Astral projecting right before you fall asleep is a great opportunity to learn how to astral project, because you will naturally be in a relaxed state. However, it is important that you refrain from attempting to astral project while you sleep, unless you are willing to learn how to safely engage in lucid dreaming. If you are not yet ready or skilled in this particular form of astral projection, you may find yourself having intense, overwhelming, or even traumatic dreams because they are so vivid. Controlling your astral experiences in a dream state is far more challenging than doing it when you are somewhat awake, so it is advised that you avoid astral projection or travel during your dreams, until you know what you are doing.

The best opportunity to engage in astral projection around your sleep is during the "twilight hour" or when you are just starting to fall asleep. At this point, you are not actually asleep yet, though you are far less connected to the present state of reality than you normally would be. This means it is far easier for you to disconnect and let go, allowing yourself to fully project into your astral self.

When doing an astral projection before you fall asleep, it can be helpful to have a small alarm that sounds after a set period of time so you can wake up from your astral projection and then intentionally go to bed.

As you prepare to do your astral projection before falling asleep, make sure you are comfortable. You will want to refrain from moving your physical body, as any movements will draw you out of the astral projection experience. Instead, you want to stay as close to still as possible. To help you stay still, you want to ensure that you are comfortable, laying in a position you can maintain, have blankets to help you maintain the right temperature, and that you will not be distracted until your alarm goes off. You can do this by shutting off your electronics, ensuring no one interrupts you, and keeping the lights down low. If you have a large amount of background noise in your space, you might like to play some calm music, or listen to music through noise-canceling headphones, so you are less likely to be distracted by the world around you. The less distracted you are, the less likely your physical senses will be to draw you back into your physical body. Understand that even if you are typically a heavy sleeper, the process of astral projecting does *not* put you into a proper state of sleep, so you will not experience that same soundness during an astral projection experience. Take the necessary steps to keep yourself from being distracted so you can enjoy your experience with zero interruptions.

Once you have set the environment, you can start your astral projection experience. To do this, allow yourself to first focus on falling into a deeper state of relaxation, as though you were about to fall asleep. However, keep your mental awareness alert. Your body will begin to grow heavy, and you will feel your breath slowing down as you begin to enter a deeper state of relaxation. It will take some effort to keep your mind awake for at least 20 minutes after your last movement so that your body is fully still, but your mind is active and ready to astral project. At that point, you can start setting your intention for your astral projection. You might focus on simply going out of your body, or moving around the room you are physically in. You might even astral project and focus on engaging in an energy healing on your astral body, if you so desire. At this point, you can do whatever it is you desire. Allow yourself to explore this state of astral projection, following your desired intentions, until your alarm goes off or you are ready to awaken yourself from your astral projection. If you find you are ready to awaken prior to your alarm going off, simply move your astral body back into your physical body and awaken yourself. You will come out of that state and find yourself back in the physical room, interacting with the physical world around you using your human body, rather than your astral body.

Chapter 7: How to Perform Astral Travel

Because astral travel is different from astral projection, it is important that you prepare yourself for this experience. Astral travel will require more effort on your behalf, and it requires more protection since you will be moving your astral body through the astral realms, which leaves you more susceptible to coming into contact with other energies. It is important that you keep your personal energy shielded, and that you ground and cleanse upon returning, to avoid having any unwanted energies attach to yours and wreak havoc in your life. If you do come back from an astral travel experience and feel as though something has attached itself to you, a simple grounding and cleansing meditation should be plenty to release it, so long as you hold your intention strong. Trust in yourself and your ability to keep yourself and your energy safe, and lean into the experience.

Using a Specific Object to Travel

One way that people astral travel is by using a specific object that stimulates their experience. The object is used as a way to connect to the energy of the location or realm they want to travel to, providing them with an "in" or a key to that energy field. While this is not necessary, many feel as though they have stronger abilities and greater accuracy when using an object to assist them with their astral travel journeys.

The object you choose for your journey can be just about anything, so long as it correlates with the energy of the location you want to travel to.

Examples include:

- Someone's belonging, if you want to astral travel to their time period to gain information about them or the time period

- Someone's belonging, if you want to astral travel to them right now and ensure they are ok or find out information about them

- A crystal that represents a certain realm or location if you want to astral travel to that realm or location to receive information (ex. moldavite to communicate with extraterrestrials, or lemurian to communicate with Lemuria through astral travel)

- An amulet that represents a certain place (such as a meeting zone where you can meet your spirit guides)

- A picture, handwritten letter, trinket, or object that connects you to a certain person, era, or energy

When you have the item in your possession, you can use it by meditating with it. Generally speaking, you will follow a standard meditation practice to enter the astral plane with your astral body, but you will keep the object near to your physical body so you can "bring" its energies with you. Then, in the astral realm, you can tap into that energy and use it as a portal to get to exactly where you desire to go in that realm.

If you intend on using an object to help you with astral projection, it is imperative that you are confident in the energy associated with that object. Always cleanse an object before or after use, even if it is only a picture or a handwritten letter, as they can carry with them many different energies. Cleansing the energy ensures you do not accidentally travel to unwanted realms, get in contact with unsafe energies, or bring an entity or energy into your life that requires intense cleansing efforts to shield yourself. Just as you would cleanse your own energy when you return from your venture, you should cleanse the energy of the object, too, since you interacted with it in the astral realm and directed its energy in a specific way.

To cleanse your object, you can use a combination of intention with smoke cleansing, or you can use moonlight to help you stimulate a cleansing experience. If you use smoke cleansing, burn sage incense and pass the object through the smoke, visualizing it purifying and cleansing the object. If you want to use moonlight to cleanse the object, leave the object out under the moon for one full moon cycle, meaning you want to place it out on the eve of a full moon and leave it there until the following full moon.

Never sleep with the object near your bed, as it could interrupt your sleeping habits and stimulate vivid or unwanted dream experiences. It is best to store objects in a box or sachet in a room separate to where you sleep, and to only bring that particular object out when you intend on working with it to avoid having your energies interact in an unwanted manner.

Following a Guided Meditation

Like with astral projection, guided meditations can be an excellent way to astral travel. Again, you will require greater focus, strength, and consistency to astral travel through your meditation because of the amount of energy it requires to do so, as well as the amount of energy you will interact with when you are in the astral realm.

To begin your astral projection, you want to start by relaxing your body completely. Ideally, you should sit up and stay in an engaged position for this, as this allows you to keep yourself consciously alert and aware of what is going on. Ensure that your body is able to rest in your engaged position, so you are able to release your physical experience for the duration of your astral travel. Generally, sitting in a cross-legged position with your hands resting on your thighs, palms up, and your spine straight with your head forward is the best engaged position to hold. This ensures you are comfortable and able to remain still for as long as you need.

Once you feel comfortable, you can start focusing on your breath. Be careful and intentional at this point, and focus on your breath, drawing a figure eight through your body and into the core of the earth. One loop of the figure eight should course through your body, while the other loop should course through the earth. The cross in the center of the figure eight should occur about two feet below your tailbone. As you inhale, visualize the energy looping around through you and down into the center of the earth, and as you exhale, visualize the energy looping through the center of the earth and back up through you. Set the intention for this grounding energy cycle to continue to remain in place for as long as you are astral traveling, as it will help keep your energy pure and focused.

After several moments, when you start to feel deeply grounded and connected, allow yourself to release. Feel yourself physically releasing from your body and allowing yourself to move into the astral realm. To do this, spend time visualizing your astral body removing itself from your physical body. Do not rush this process or attempt to force it. Both rush and force will prevent you from being able to fully release.

Once you have officially released, set the intention of where you want to go. Be patient, again, as you allow yourself to get there. Follow any path that presents itself to you on the way, as it is unlikely to look like any physical path from this reality. You might be drawn down a path that resembles a physical path, or you might be drawn down a channel, an energy path, or any other number of paths to get yourself to your destination.

At this point, you can follow your intuition and allow yourself to engage in the desired realm and area for as long as you desire. You can visit, look for information, ask questions, engage with the realm around you, or even seek to bring certain energies back with you. For example, if you are seeking more joy, you might travel into a realm of purity and bring back the energy of joy with you to help you experience more joy in your life.

When you are ready to remove yourself from the astral realm, go ahead and travel back to your physical body. When you arrive, visualize yourself moving back into your physical body and begin moving your physical body so you can awaken yourself from the astral travel experience. Spend several more moments in the figure-8 grounded breathing experience so you can ground your energies and release any unwanted energies from your trip.

Astral Traveling in Your Sleep

Astral travel is something you can do while you sleep, though it is not something you should do until you are comfortable with astral projection *and* astral travel during your meditations. With sleep, you will likely be venturing into the astral realm for a prolonged period of time, and you will be even more detached from your physical body than you are during your meditation, so you need to be ready to bring yourself back if and when you need to.

The best way to engage in astral travel when you sleep is to do so during a nap, as astral traveling when you are attempting to sleep through the night can result in you having vivid dreams and restless sleep. In the end, you might find yourself struggling with symptoms of exhaustion, and possibly overwhelm from the adventure you have, as an all-night astral travel journey can be excessive, especially for a new practitioner.

If you want to try astral traveling during your sleep, set an alarm for at least one and a half hours after you start, and no more than three hours. Remember, it will take time to actually reach your astral travel state, so you need to account for that. Otherwise, you will wake up too early into your journey. Set the alarm based on the journey you are taking and what you want to experience on that journey.

When you are ready, lay down and ensure that you are completely comfortable. Use a pillow, and cover yourself with a blanket, so you maintain a comfortable temperature, and eliminate any distractions. Then, start your session by closing your eyes, and engaging in a rhythmic breathing exercise. As with astral projection, you want to allow your entire body to fall asleep while keeping your conscious mind awake and engaged. You can do this by remaining as still as possible, which will allow your body to fall asleep. Through this process, you will feel your limbs growing heavy and your breath slowing, and you will find yourself enjoying a deeper sense of relaxation as you go.

Around about twenty minutes after you have relaxed, your body will be asleep, and you will be able to engage in the process of projecting your astral body out of your physical body. Spend as much time as you need here, allowing your astral body to be released from your physical body. When you feel fully released, set the intention of where you want to go and follow the path to get there. As you arrive, you can explore, engage with, or receive whatever it is you need from this space. Spend as much time as you need or want here before returning back to your physical body to wake up.

If you are astral traveling during sleep, know that your alarm will pull you back to your physical body and wake you up, so if you are not done by the time your alarm goes off, you will be pulled back. This is an important protective measure, however, especially for early adventures, so do not avoid the alarm in fear of running out of time. Instead, consider setting the alarm for a little longer if you need to, so that you can finish your experience. It should also be noted that astral travel during sleep will be much easier for you to access if you already have experience with lucid dreaming. If you struggle to have an astral travel experience in your sleep, learning how to lucid dream might be something you would like to pursue.

Chapter 8: Coming Back to Your Body

Coming back to your physical body after an astral projection or astral travel experience is not as simple as just waking up. While this is part of it, there are additional steps you need to take to ensure that you awaken to the room around you in a way that allows you to soundly engage in the physical realm once more. People who awaken and attempt to immediately go back to their daily life will often find themselves feeling "off" or even out of touch with the world around them, to the point where it may make astral traveling seem scary or uncertain. Fortunately, this can be avoided or resolved by following a few necessary steps to come back to your body properly.

What Happens When You Come Back?

When you come back from an astral experience, your physical body will not feel quite the same. Immediately upon reintegrating, you will find yourself feeling as though you are walking on clouds, or like you are somehow disconnected from your body. Some people report feeling as though they are watching themselves from above, or like the world around them is lacking a certain "realness" that makes it feel as though they are removed from their physical experience. This occurs when you come back into your physical body but fail to merge your astral and physical experience as one.

It is important to understand that the reintegration may take longer if you are new to astral projection or astral travel. It can also take longer than usual if you spend too much time in the astral realm, as your astral body grows used to being disconnected from your physical body. For this reason, it is important to give yourself adequate time to reintegrate after an astral experience.

If you find yourself not properly integrating with your body, take as long as you need to move through the steps of integration. If you still cannot seem to reintegrate, consider grounding outside with the physical earth, or having an energy work session done, such as Reiki. Do not reengage in any astral experiences until you have fully reintegrated and been integrated for at least a week. After that, keep your experiences short to avoid overdoing it. Start slow and take short trips as you practice the skill of reintegrating. That way, you will avoid having any traumatic experiences associated with disconnection or failure to reintegrate.

Keeping Track of Your Astral Experiences

As soon as you wake up from your astral journey, write about it in your journal. Once you have finished your reintegration, you might forget key pieces of your journey, or energies you experienced, similarly to how you quickly forget dreams upon waking. Write everything out authentically and objectively, and copy down as much as you possibly can. Do not review any of this information, attempt to interpret it or understand it, or judge it in any way for now. Your sole goal is to brain dump everything onto the page so you can maintain as much of the information as possible.

It is a good idea to keep your astral journal for astral journeys exclusively and to keep it nearby anytime you go into the astral realm, whether you are projecting or traveling. You will not want to immediately stand up and start walking around after a session, as doing so can result in you actually making it harder to reintegrate. Immediately after coming back, you will want to stay still and relax for a few minutes, as this will drastically improve your reintegration experience.

Awakening into Each of Your Senses

Once you have brain dumped your entire experience into your journal, you need to awaken into each of your senses. This process is an important part of reintegrating as it merges your physical senses with your astral body once again, ensuring they are not operating independently of each other. It is when these senses all operate independently of each other that you find yourself feeling disconnected.

With your sense of touch, touch as many different textures as you possibly can. The more you touch, the more you will reintegrate as you will be experiencing a number of different sensations. Make sure everything you touch is pleasurable and not dangerous.

For your sense of sound, start focusing on the sounds around you and seeing if you can identify where they are coming from. Spending time focusing on where sounds are coming from, and what they are, helps you use your mind in the physical realm, which allows you to reintegrate more effectively.

Reintegrate your sense of sight by looking around to see as many different objects as you possibly can. As you look at each object, describe it to yourself by identifying it and then describing what it looks like, and any interesting details you notice about it. Describe at least five different objects to ensure you spend adequate time becoming reintegrated with your sense of sight.

For your sense of smell, pick up objects nearby and begin smelling them so you can become aware of what the different scents are. Smell candles, incense, your clothes, your hands, and anything else you wish to smell as a way to bring yourself back into your body. Again, describe what it is, become aware of how it smells, and consider what the smell feels like for you.

With your sense of taste, consider drinking freshwater, a sip of juice, or having a small snack to reintegrate into your physical body. Keeping a drink or snack nearby ensures that upon awakening, you can drink or eat without having to get up and search for food. Be mindful of your experience by becoming aware of what it is you are eating or drinking, how it feels in your mouth, what it tastes like, and whether or not you are enjoying it.

Be as mindful as possible as you reintegrate each of your physical senses, as your mindfulness will help draw your energy and awareness back into your physical body. This way, your senses all reintegrate properly, and you find yourself fully connected with the present experience once more. Be patient in this process and give yourself as much time as you need to come back, as rushing this could lead to you attempting to go back to daily life while still experiencing a sense of disconnect. If after focusing on each one of your senses you don't feel fully reintegrated, a mindfulness meditation practice can be particularly helpful.

Grounding and Cleansing Your Energy Field

After you have reintegrated your senses, you need to ground and cleanse your energy field. You want to do this after you have reintegrated your physical senses, as it ensures that you work with your energy from your physical point of consciousness, too. Through this, you will deepen your reintegration process and bring yourself further back into your physical body. Further, it cleanses your energy from both your physical body and your astral body, helping to reintegrate you back into your physical experience.

To ground your energy, it is best to sit upright and connect your tailbone to the earth. Visualize your root chakra growing a root out into the center of the earth and use that root to help you release the energy that you have in your body. See all of the energy in your body coursing down through the root and coming back into your body through the root, purified and released from any unwanted energies that may have attached themselves to you.

Once you have completed the grounding process, visualize a golden ball of energy forming in the center of your body at your solar plexus chakra. As you inhale, visualize it growing stronger and brighter, and as you exhale, visualize the ball expanding out and removing any energies you do not want from your space. Continue doing this until the golden shield of light expands out beyond your body and surrounds you like a large, golden egg protecting you within its energy field. Once your shield reaches the maximum size, you should feel complete relief from any energies that were not yours, as well as balanced in all of your energy that remains. Feel free to relax here as long as you desire, so long as you remain consciously engaged with the physical, present moment to avoid slipping back into an astral state.

Integrating into Your Daily Experiences

Even when you are done integrating back into your physical body, chances are you will find yourself feeling a sense of disconnect. If you are new to astral experiences, or if you went on a rather large journey, it is not unusual to feel somewhat out of it for the rest of the day. It is best to plan your astral journeying on days when you can take it slow and do low-commitment activities, so you are not obligated to try to push through anything too strenuous when you are feeling off. Spend the rest of the day taking it easy, going slow, and giving yourself the space to enjoy the day.

Aside from taking it easy, ensure that you take excellent care of your body. Eat healthy, nourishing meals that replenish all of your energy. It is best to eat foods with all the colors of the rainbow, as this will nourish all of your chakras. You should also do some gentle exercise, such as a yoga session, and ensure that you get a good sleep that night. All of these measures ensure that you reintegrate effectively and that you recover from your astral travel experience. The more you get into a healthy reintegration routine, the easier it will be to reintegrate after any further astral projection or travel journeys that you take.

Chapter 9: Crystals, Essential Oils, and Mantras

When it comes to astral projection and travel, there are many crystals, essential oils, and other tools you can use to help you on your journey. Mantras, for example, work as a wonderful opportunity to align your energy and your intentions and keep yourself prepared for the experience that lies ahead. Each of these tools has its own way of being incorporated into your experience, so be sure you fully understand them before using them.

Crystal for Astral Projection and Travel

There are many different crystals you can use to assist you with your astral journeys. Crystals can be worn, kept under your pillow, held against your body, or kept nearby as a way to either aid in your ability to release yourself from your physical body, venture seamlessly through the astral realms, or protect yourself during your journey. Avoid using too many different crystals at once, as this could result in you experiencing overwhelming energies and having an uncomfortable experience. Instead, use one for astral travel, and one for protection, at most.

Amethyst

Amethyst is known for protecting the third eye, while aiding in having positive, effective third eye experiences. Since astral projections and travels incorporate the "unseen" realms, this crystal works wonderfully as both an assistant and a protective stone when you are astral projecting or traveling.

Angel Aura Quartz

Angel aura quartz is a crystal of the higher realms, and it assists with higher communications. You can use angel aura quartz as a way to tap into higher realms, especially those associated with angels and spirit guides. This crystal will provide you guidance, but it will not provide you with protection.

Black Obsidian

Black obsidian is a powerful protective stone. It will absorb negative energies and deflect any unwanted entities away from yourself and your physical and spiritual bodies, effectively keeping you safe during and after your journey. During the grounding and cleansing process, hold black obsidian in your hand to help eliminate any unwanted energies from your field.

Blue Calcite

Blue calcite is a stone associated with your throat chakra; it can speak to your ability to communicate within the higher realms. If you are going into the higher realms to retrieve information or guidance, you can use blue calcite to help you with that mission.

Jasper

Jasper is an excellent protection stone during astral projection or travel. You can use jasper to help ground you back into your physical body or connect to your physical energies after an astral journey. When you have returned, use jasper as a way to ground yourself from the energies, too.

Lemurian

Lemurian is a crystal that is associated with the ancient continent of Lemuria, which sunk many years ago. If you desire to communicate with an ancient colony to retrieve information from them, you can use lemurian during your astral travel to assist you with getting where you want to go, and receiving the desired information.

Moldavite

Moldavite is known for connecting people to extraterrestrial energies. If you want to communicate with extraterrestrial energies, carrying a piece of moldavite on your astral journey is an excellent idea. Be sure to carry a protective stone like black obsidian with you, too, however, as there are infinite energies and entities in the extraterrestrial realms, and you never know what you may encounter.

Essential Oils for a Safe Journey

Essential oils that correspond with your third eye chakra and crown chakra are best for astral projection or traveling because they help activate the two chakras that are most closely related to the astral realms. The essential oils you can bring with you include oils like mugwort, blue lotus, kava kava, rosemary, lavender, and sage. Juniper, white lotus, frankincense, myrrh, cedarwood, rosewood, chamomile, sandalwood, white neroli, and vanilla are also great for these chakras and will aid you in having a strong astral experience.

When you are coming back into your body, you want to use essential oils that cater to your root chakra. These oils will aid in grounding you and releasing any unwanted energies from your field as you connect closely to the earth. Nutmeg, patchouli, and bergamot are great for grounding your energy field. Vetiver can also be used, as this is another deeply grounding essential oil.

When using essential oils, be sure to either diffuse them or dilute them properly to avoid accidentally overdosing yourself and your field with these oils. They can be too strong if they are not properly diffused or diluted, which can lead to accidental illness or injury if you are not careful.

Mantras to Set Your Intentions

Having a mantra to set your intentions is a great way to keep your energy field strong. With mantras, you can repeat the mantra over and over, giving yourself something finite to focus on and hold onto as you travel. Choose your mantra before going into the journey so that you can repeat the mantra throughout it. If you need to, infuse your mantra with intention beforehand so you can gain the most from this phrase.

A few good mantras to set your intention include:

- "I will have a safe, productive journey into the astral realm."

- "My energy will remain sovereign and free of interference."

- "I will effortlessly ground and cleanse from this experience."

- "I am going to receive the guidance I need."

- "I freely release myself from my physical body for a safe, enjoyable experience."

- "I am enjoying the astral realm."

- "I release myself from my physical duties, so I can find the answers I seek."

- "I receive only that which serves my highest good and the highest good of all."

- "I decide what comes into my energy field, and without my direct and exact permission, nothing comes through."

- "I am enjoying a positive, safe experience."

You can also make your own mantra. To make your own mantra for astral travel, first think of what it is that you desire to experience, then consider a short mantra you could use to affirm that desired experience. It is a good idea to write this mantra down on paper and meditate on the mantra itself. Always be sure that your language is clear and precise and declares exactly what you desire, as inconsistencies in your language can lead to you not having your desired experience.

Amulets, Talismans, and Tools for Journeying

Amulets, talismans, and tools can be useful for astral journeying, too. Amulets are tools you can make, whereas talismans are tools you can find. Each tool will have its own unique method for being incorporated into astral journeying, whether they be to enhance your ability to project or travel, or to protect you on your journey. Some may also be designed to connect you with specific energies, such as your spirit guides or guardian angels. Know that amulets, talismans, and other tools will always be highly personal to you, so it is best to meditate with these tools to understand how to use them, care for them, and protect them. This way, you have a personal, productive relationship with these tools.

Chapter 10: Astral Projecting
with Friends

One of the more advanced practices of astral projection and astral travel is to learn how to do this with friends. When you learn how to astral project with your friends, you gain the ability to share a unique and enjoyable experience. This can also make your journey more powerful. For example, if you are both seeking specific information, you can work together to gain that information from the astral realms, possibly increasing the amount of value you gain from your efforts. You also enjoy the bond that comes from sharing this experience together, as well as the increased energetic powers that come from learning how to connect with another human in the astral realms.

Astral Projecting Together

Before you can astral project with anyone else, you need to know how to astral project by yourself. You should feel confident in astral projecting or traveling, as well as coming back to your body and grounding and cleansing your energies. You should experiment with taking a journey similar to that which you will take with your friend on your own, first, as this ensures that you will be confident doing it with your friend. Your friend should also be comfortable journeying on their own, to ensure you are both bringing intentional, confident, and productive energies on your journey.

For the process of journeying together, you do not have to physically be in the same space, though this may work as a way to increase your powers on earth. This also gives you the opportunity to discuss your experience after you are done so you can share your unique interpretations and discover what they mean. It is important that you follow your own unique method for astral journeying and reintegrating with your body upon coming back, and that you do not try to follow your friend, as you are accustomed to your method. This method has worked for you in the past, and it will continue to work reliably for you now, too. If you stray away or leave the process incomplete, you could end your session feeling out of sorts.

Creating Shared Experiences

To create shared astral journeying experiences with your friends, you need to have a clear idea of where you are going, what you are doing there, and how you can connect with each other. Having one friend arrive first and the second meet the first friend there is the best way to draw your energies close together. You should both hold the intention of attracting and finding your friend in the astral realm if you want to effectively find each other.

It can help to use an object that belongs to your friend to channel their energy and guide your astral self toward them. Swapping a piece of jewelry, a picture, or even a crystal with your friend is a great way to connect your energies together and magnetically attract each other as you embark on your journey. Continue manifesting the attraction of your friend until you can fully feel their presence with you, never leaving before you entirely sense it. Because time works differently in the astral realms than it does in the physical realms, you might arrive and journey at different physical times, but you both can arrive at exactly the same time, technically.

Sensing the Energy of Your Friends

Sensing the energy of your friend in the astral realm is easier to do if you are already familiar with the energy of your friend in the physical realm. If you are not best friends who spend ample amounts of time together, it can be helpful to first meditate on each other's energy and spend time together, so you become familiar with each other and used to each other. If either of you practices energy work or psychic sessions, you could do sessions with each other as a way to become more familiar with each other's energy. Once you reach the astral realm, your first order of business is to locate that exact energy that you have become familiar with.

Going on Astral Traveling Journeys

It is best if you plan an "itinerary" beforehand, so you are not in the astral realm wondering what to do or where to go. Your itinerary might include specific places you want to go or specific information or energies you want to attract. As soon as you have fully connected with your friend's energy, you want to embark on the journey that you agreed upon. At this point, you can focus more on the journey than on merging your energies, since you have already done this part. However, you may want to check in with your friend's energy every so often to ensure they are still nearby, and you are still together. If you ever find that you can no longer sense your friend's presence, pause and attract their energy back to you once more so you can venture together again. Once you have attracted them back into your energy field, you can continue on your adventure.

Keeping Your Energy Independent

When you hang out with someone in the physical realm, it is only natural that your bodies remain separate. After all, there are physical barriers protecting you from merging with your friend and becoming "one." In the astral realm, the lack of physical barriers can result in your energies accidentally merging too much. It is important that you attract your friend's energy and merge with them, without actually becoming one. This means that while your energies are linked, they do not become a new energy that essentially creates a codependency between your astral bodies. Keep your energy independent with strong boundaries, intention, and the desire to journey together, not as a single entity but as a team. By keeping your boundaries and intentions strong, you can assist yourself with staying sovereign during your journey. It also helps to cleanse your energies and intentionally remove your friend's energy from your energy field as soon as you arrive back in your physical body to ensure they are not lingering in your space. They should do the same.

Protecting Yourself During Your Journey

When you venture as a team on earth, there is a notion that "no man is left behind." In the astral realm, this cannot be the case. Each of you needs to be responsible for your own personal energies. You should use your own shields, your own forms of protection, and your own intentions to ensure that your energy is protected and safe. Envision that you are taking two independent trips side by side, rather than venturing as a team that protects and drives one another's experience. This way, you can both remain responsible for your own energies. Attempting to protect each other can actually be incredibly exhausting and can make coming back into your physical bodies extremely challenging. Stick with what you know, and trust each other to take the necessary steps to protect yourselves during the journey. If you come back into the physical realm and find that someone has had an unwanted energy or entity attach themselves to that individual, focus on creating healing there, not in the astral realm.

Reflecting on Your Astral Adventure

Once you and your friend have both awoke from your astral adventure, you need to discuss that adventure. This should happen after you have individually journaled and come back into your physical bodies to avoid being kept in the disconnected state. When you have completely reintegrated into your physical bodies, you can compare your journals and your experiences from there.

When you start to compare your journeys, you might notice that you do not both share the exact same journey memories. For example, you might have seen different things, spoken to different people, experienced different energies, or brought back different information from your journeys. This occurs, not because you did not effectively meet up, but because you are both experiencing the astral realms through your own personal filters. The astral realms present themselves to you in a way that your conscious, human mind understands, which means that the filter you see through and the filter your friend sees through will be entirely different. To gain the most out of your journeys, relay your experiences, and discuss what these energies meant for you and the messages you have taken away. More often than not, your messages will be similar or will work together to create the entire message you were seeking.

Conclusion

Congratulations on completing this book on astral projection!

This book was written to help you discover the mysterious world of astral projection, and to safely and effectively tap into it. Learning how to astral project, or astral travel, is an exciting adventure that can bring with it many unique experiences and pieces of information. You can do anything from enjoying the experience of separate realms, to receiving specific guidance and support from your spirit guides, universal energies, or other entities in the astral realms. There are many benefits you can gain from this skill, which makes it a wonderful one for anyone to learn.

I hope that through reading this book, you have discovered how to safely and effectively travel the astral realms. It is vital that you respect these realms and the energies they contain. Remember that in realms beyond earth, there are many energies and entities, and not all of them are pure or kind-hearted. I do not say this to scare you; I say this to remind you of the importance of taking these journeys seriously and fully grounding and cleansing your energies when you return. Having proper protection as you go into the realms and conducting adequate grounding and cleansing afterwards is plenty to ensure you have a safe experience.

I strongly encourage you to begin enjoying your own astral projecting and astral traveling adventures. Discover what your unique experiences are like, find your own signature rituals for releasing into your astral body, and coming back into your physical body, and learn to become comfortable with the entire experience. The more you expose yourself and practice healthy, effective habits for enjoying the astral realm, the more you stand to gain from your experiences.

I also encourage you to keep a thorough journal of your experiences. Not only will this help you reflect on each individual adventure, but it will also help you look back through your experiences and recall them at a later date. You never know when a past astral journey will bring forth information that will help your future self!

Once again, I'd like to thank you for choosing this book. I hope that you enjoyed it!

CPSIA information can be obtained
at www.ICGtesting.com
Printed in the USA
BVHW041114131020
590916BV00011B/763

9 781761 0356